I

II

# QUICK & SIMPLE RECORD KEEPING SYSTEM
## FOR
## OWNER/OPERATORS

# QUICK & SIMPLE RECORD KEEPING SYSTEM FOR OWNER/OPERATORS

Copyright ©2005
Timothy D. Brady & Esta Klatzkin

Published by Write Up The Road
P.O. Box 69
Kenton, Tennessee 38233
**www.writeuptheroad.com**

ISBN: 0-9724026-8-3
Printed in the United States of America

**A Truckers' University Book**

# FOREWORD

It is a common saying in business that the life-blood of any business is cash flow. If that is true, then financial information about the business is the nerve system. And, like the nerve system of a body, a business must gather a diverse and seemingly endless amount of pieces of information; gather in one central location, summarize it, analyze the summarized information and then take appropriate action to protect it from harm.

This book is about how to gather, summarize and report the information of your business so that you can take the action required to maximize your profits.

In all of my years of practicing public accounting, I have never encountered an industry more in need of a "how to" manual to accomplish the task of gathering, summarizing and reporting financial information than the trucking industry and, more specifically, the Owner/Operator who owns and operates a single truck.

If you are an Owner/Operator who is serious about your business, but need guidance on how to set-up and maintain a simple record keeping system that requires a minimal amount of your time and effort to maintain, this is the book for which you have been waiting.

The goal in writing it was not to make you an expert in accounting and tax, but to provide you with the tool you need to organize and safeguard your business records so that you or your business counselors will have the information you need to make decisions about your business.

–John Turner, CPA
The Trucker's Accountant

# INTRODUCTION

The information in this manual can change your world – or at least your bank account!.

The next logical step should be to investigate and understand the "system." The "system" is larger than all of us. It has been around for a long time. It is a big, powerful and volatile system, and most importantly, you can't circumvent or beat it – but you can win <u>with</u> the system!

I'm sure you know that most of us are working twice as hard as our parents did, yet we have less to show for it. Of course, we are earning more, but inflation has caused our dollars to be worth less.

Every year the private research organization Tax Foundation, calculates "Tax Freedom Day;" that symbolic point in the year when all the income earned by the average American taxpayer no longer goes to pay federal, state, and local taxes. As you can imagine, the day arrives later each year.

There has never been a more urgent time to learn how to legally reduce your taxes!

When looking for an accountant or tax expert here are a few things you should be looking for:

1. Don't be creatively crippled: be sure your accountant or tax preparer knows the nuances of trucking.
2. Find an expert that knows how to form deductions, not one that just puts deductions on forms.
3. Be sure they have an office that is active in truckers' accounting 24/7/365; you don't need a "Tax Season Wonder" (someone who puts their tax shingle up in January and takes it down April 15).
4. Are they licensed to practice before the Internal Revenue Service as your representative?
5. Are they a licensed CPA (Certified Public Accountant) or an E.A. (Enrolled Agent)?
6. Is the majority of their business Truck Owner/Operators?
7. Do they know what the Meals per Diem allowed by the IRS is for truckers (as of 2005, it is 75% of $42.00)?

This manual contains no assumptions, speculation, or postulations but rather tried, tested, and proven approaches, techniques, methods, and strategies for **legally and ethically** reducing one's income tax through small business deductions. In fact, all of the business deductions are supported by the tax code, Treasury rulings, IRS regulations, and court decisions!

The primary reason for being in business

should be to make money. Tax benefits accompanying the business should be viewed as a secondary by-product. These deductions are legally given to you as incentives to get into business and stay there, because when you are spending money to build your business, you are stimulating the economy and protecting and creating jobs. Because Uncle Sam likes a vibrant economy resulting in fewer people on unemployment and welfare rolls, he rewards you, the small businessperson, with a myriad of tax write-offs. The plan to help the economy is a return to free-enterprise principles with less government and more tax breaks for investors and businesses. Calvin Coolidge knew that "The business of America is business."

This manual contains many hard-to-find tips and strategies not generally known to the public, which will certainly cut your taxes. If you're really serious about reducing your taxes, the time and energy you invest in recordkeeping and planning is the key to success. The basic deductions and principles in this manual should be timeless, lending you foundational support for many years to come. This manual will be handy to read at the beginning, middle, and end of the year and will help you keep your accountant on his or her toes – and perhaps even to light a fire under him or her!

Wishing You, Many Happy Returns!–
**–Esta Klatzkin, Enrolled Agent**

# CONTENTS

# CHAPTER ONE

## QUICK & SIMPLE RECORD KEEPING SYSTEM

## ITEMS YOU'LL NEED

Congratulations, you are now beginning your drive on the highway to financial success. In this chapter, you'll be provided the list of items necessary to quickly and simply keep track of all those pesky, but valuable cash receipts. Receipts: those small but significant slips of paper are swallowed by the sleeper, or lie on the dash and become faded to a point of uselessness.

The plan is to take up as little space as possible with a system that requires no more than five minutes per day and half an hour at the end of each week to accumulate, categorize, add and permanently file those receipts.

**Remember:** *Every dollar of every receipt correctly categorized, added and filed represents a 40¢ reduction in your income taxes. (That's $40 for every $100 in receipts which are properly filed!)*

The items listed on the following pages are readily available at any office supply store, large discount store, or online. Pictures have been included to make locating the correct components of the Quick & Simple Record Keeping System easy.

Oh, yes, remember to save the receipt from your purchase of these items - it's a tax deductible expense to be filed under *Category 15 Office Expense.*

**Quick & Simple Expense Receipt File Box:**

The first item you will need is a large, portable File Box. This File Box is the permanent place for all your Trucking Business Receipts. In this File Box you will keep your **Expanding Laminated Receipt Wallet**, Expense Category File Jackets, and all the necessary forms and tools to maintain your Quick & Simple Record Keeping System. *Keep this File Box in a safe place, as this is where your receipts will remain permanently.*

**3½" Expansion, Colored Expanding Laminated Wallet**

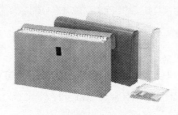

As your business day progresses and you purchase different Business Related Items, it is <u>very</u> important that you get a receipt for that purchase. Each time you return to your truck, put all your receipts into this Expanding Laminated

Wallet. If you are not able to get a receipt, jot down the date, amount and short description of what you purchased on a page from a small note pad and put it in the Expanding Laminated Wallet with your other receipts.

**Expense Category File Jackets**

 There are 30 different Standard Expense Categories. But, you'll need at least 40 Expense Category File Jackets, one for each of the 30 Standard Expense Categories, plus some extras for additional expense categories that are unique to your business. Please note that each Category has a Number, (1 through 30) which is the ACCOUNT NUMBER to each corresponding Standard Expense Category (#1 Bank Charges, #30 Vehicle Leases, etc). We recommend you get 40 to 50 of these file jackets. (If you don't use them this year, you'll need them next year.) These become your permanent files for your expense receipts.

## Pocket Calculator

Keep it simple; all you'll need to do is some addition at the end of each week.

## Mechanical Pencils

A good Mechanical pencil is essential. Buy the less expensive ones by the dozen. It's a lot cheaper than having to keep track of spare leads and you don't end up with wood pencil shavings all over the inside of your cab.

## Fluorescent Highlighters

A Higntlighter Pen or two is essential. You will use these to help you categorize each expense receipt for proper filing.

## #10 White Business Envelopes

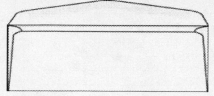

You need a box of #10 Business Envelopes to place your sorted and totaled expense receipts in your permanent file each month.
(You'll write on each envelope the Expense Category Code # and Expense Category Name.)

## 3M Scotch® Retractable Glue Stick

You will also need a retractable glue stick to attach your Quick & Simple Expense Category Tracker Forms to the outside of your file jackets.

# QUICK & SIMPLE
## Expense Category Tracker Forms

| CATEGORY | CLIENTS NAME | | | | ACCT # | | CODE# | |
|---|---|---|---|---|---|---|---|---|
| YEAR_____ | 1ST WEEK TOTAL | 2ND WEEK TOTAL | 3RD WEEK TOTAL | 4TH WEEK TOTAL | | MONTHS TOTAL | | |
| January | | | | | | | | |
| February | | | | | | | | |
| March | | | | | | | | |
| April | | | | | | | | |
| May | | | | | | | | |
| June | | | | | | | | |
| July | | | | | | | | |
| August | | | | | | | | |
| September | | | | | | | | |
| October | | | | | | | | |
| November | | | | | | | | |
| December | | | | | | | | |

These are the forms on which you'll be entering the totals from the receipts that fit into each of the 30 different categories. You will attach one form to each of your 30 Standard Expense Category File Jackets using the glue stick. Place the glue on all 4 backside edges of each form. Then place the glued form, centered, on the front of each file jacket.

# QUICK & SIMPLE
## Per Diem Lodging & Meal Log

P.R.O.F.I.T.S. PER DIEM LODGING & MEAL LOG    CLIENTS NAME_____ ACCT#_____

| | ALL CITY/STATE ENTRIES MUST CORRESPOND WITH YOUR DRIVER LOG ENTRIES FOR EACH DATE | | | | | | | |
|---|---|---|---|---|---|---|---|---|
| DATE | CITY/STATE WHERE SLEPT | HOME | SLEEPER | OTHER PLACE | MEALS | LODGING | |
| 1 | | | | | | | 1 |
| 2 | | | | | | | 2 |
| 3 | | | | | | | 3 |
| 4 | | | | | | | 4 |
| 5 | | | | | | | 5 |
| 6 | | | | | | | 6 |
| 7 | | | | | | | 7 |
| 8 | | | | | | | 8 |
| 9 | | | | | | | 9 |
| 10 | | | | | | | 10 |
| 11 | | | | | | | 11 |
| 12 | | | | | | | 12 |
| 13 | | | | | | | 13 |
| 14 | | | | | | | 14 |
| 15 | | | | | | | 15 |
| 16 | | | | | | | 16 |
| 17 | | | | | | | 17 |
| 18 | | | | | | | 18 |
| 19 | | | | | | | 19 |
| 20 | | | | | | | 20 |
| 21 | | | | | | | 21 |
| 22 | | | | | | | 22 |
| 23 | | | | | | | 23 |
| 24 | | | | | | | 24 |
| 25 | | | | | | | 25 |
| 26 | | | | | | | 26 |
| 27 | | | | | | | 27 |
| 28 | | | | | | | 28 |
| 29 | | | | | | | 29 |
| 30 | | | | | | | 30 |
| 31 | | | | | | | 31 |

This form helps you to maximize your total available Meal and Lodging expense deductions. You'll list your final location at day's end: nearest city, county, state. You also indicate if you were at home, in the sleeper, or other location (motel, friends). And this is where you list your per diem amount for Meals and Lodging at the end of each day.

(Refer to **Chapter Five** in this book, Record Keeping for the Owner/Operator, for instructions on how to figure your per diem rates for this form.)

# QUICK & SIMPLE
## Monthly Uncategorized Expense

CLIENT_____ ACCT#_____

| DATE | ITEM PURCHASED | AMOUNT | CODE# | DATE | ITEM PURCHASED | AMOUNT | CODE# |
|---|---|---|---|---|---|---|---|
| 1 | | $ | | 16 | | $ | |
| 2 | | $ | | 17 | | $ | |
| 3 | | $ | | 18 | | $ | |
| 4 | | $ | | 19 | | $ | |
| 5 | | $ | | 20 | | $ | |
| 6 | | $ | | 21 | | $ | |
| 7 | | $ | | 22 | | $ | |
| 8 | | $ | | 23 | | $ | |
| 9 | | $ | | 24 | | $ | |
| 10 | | $ | | 25 | | $ | |
| 11 | | $ | | 26 | | $ | |
| 12 | | $ | | 27 | | $ | |
| 13 | | $ | | 28 | | $ | |
| 14 | | $ | | 29 | | $ | |
| 15 | | $ | | 30 | | $ | |

This form is for the times you just don't know in which category a particular receipt belongs. Write on this form what you purchased, the amount and the date. You will scan, fax or mail it to your bookkeeper, or accountant; for him to determine whether the item purchased is a deductible expense, and in which category it belongs. (You may also refer to **Chapter Five**, Record Keeping for the Owner/Operator, page 31 to determine the criteria for a deductible expense.)

# QUICK & SIMPLE
## Monthly Itemized Report

P.R.O.F.I.T.S. MONTHLY ITEMIZED REPORT for CLIENT_____ ACCT#_____

| CODE # | CATEGORY | # | MONTH TOTAL | # | CATEGORY | MONTH TOTAL | # |
|---|---|---|---|---|---|---|---|
| 1 | BANKING FEES | 1 | | 16 | PARKING FEES | | 16 |
| 2 | BUSINESS GIFTS ($25 Max) | 2 | | 17 | PERMITS / LICENSES / TAXES | | 17 |
| 3 | CLAIMS | 3 | | 18 | POSTAGE & SHIPPING | | 18 |
| 4 | COMMUNICATIONS | 4 | | 19 | PROFESSIONAL FEES | | 19 |
| 5 | DUES & SUBSCRIPTIONS | 5 | | 20 | SCALE TICKETS / WEIGHTS | | 20 |
| 6 | ENTERTAINMENT | 6 | | 21 | SECURITY | | 21 |
| 7 | EQUIP / NEW PURCHASE | 7 | | 22 | SHOWERS | | 22 |
| 8 | EQUIP / VEHICLE RENTAL | 8 | | 23 | TOLLS | | 23 |
| 9 | INSURANCE (Non Health) | 9 | | 24 | TOOLS | | 24 |
| 10 | INTEREST | 10 | | 25 | TRAILER EXPENSES | | 25 |
| 11 | LABOR | 11 | | 26 | TRAVEL (Airline, Bus, Train) | | 26 |
| 12 | LODGING / PER DIEM | 12 | | 27 | TRUCK / AUTO EXPENSES | | 27 |
| 13 | MAINT & REPAIR (Non Vehicle) | 13 | | 28 | TRUCK SUPPLIES | | 28 |
| 14 | MEALS / PER DIEM | 14 | | 29 | UNIFORMS / LAUNDRY | | 29 |
| 15 | OFFICE EXPENSES | 15 | | 30 | VEHICLE LEASES | | 30 |

This is the form on which you'll write the totals
from your 30 Standard Expense Category Tracker
Forms. You'll scan, fax or mail it to your
bookkeeper or your accountant; or enter totals
from here into your own bookkeeping program.

11

# How to get your Q&S Forms

You may obtain the necessary forms by going to
**www.truckersbookstore.com**,
and Clicking on:
**Q&S Record Keeping Forms**.
You may choose between a PDF Adobe Acrobat Reader®
for a free download when you register your purchase of
this book.
*Your password to open the PDF file is:*
**yth52om9it**
Or you may order them at any time by mail for $19.95
including S&H. There are a total of 72 pages of forms
plus one page of labels. If you are downloading, you'll
need a package of Avery ® 8460 labels (1" x 2 5/8"
labels, 30 per page).

**Q&S Record Keeping Category Label
Printing Instructions:**
Use **Avery®** 8460 Labels (1" X 2⅝"). Place in printer
paper feed tray according to manufacturer's instructions.
Click on **F**ile, select **P**rint. In **Page Range** section select
button for **Pages**, type the number **2** in both **From** and
**To** boxes; **Number of Copies**, select **1**; at bottom right
of Print Box click on **OK** to print.

**Q&S Record Keeping Form Printing Instructions:**
Place at least 72 sheets of 8½ X 11 paper in printer
paper feed tray according to manufacturer's instructions.
Click on **F**ile, select **P**rint. In **Page Range** section select
button for **ALL**; **Number of Copies**, select **1**; at bottom
right of Print Box click on **OK** to print.
You may also opt to copy the PDF file to a disk and take
to your local printer where you can have him print for
you.

# CHAPTER TWO

# QUICK & SIMPLE RECORD KEEPING SYSTEM

# SETTING UP

**Quick & Simple Record Keeping System Setup Instructions**

1.      Take the *Expanding Laminated Wallet* and place it inside the front of your Expense Receipt File Box. This is your central expense receipt collection point.

2.      Next take your *Quick & Simple Standard Expense Category Tracker Forms* you ordered from www.truckersbookstore.com (See NOTE at the end of Chapter 1 for instructions on how to obtain your forms and labels). Attach one form to the front of each of 30 *Standard Expense Category File Jackets*. (Place the glue on all 4 back side edges of each form. Place centered on the front of each file jacket.) Now take the first file jacket to which you have glued a *Standard Expense Category Tracker Form* and attach one Expense Category Name Label to its top edge. Repeat for each file jacket.

3.      Now place each finished *Standard Expense Category File Jacket,* in numerical order, back into the *Expense Receipt File Box.*

4.      Fill in your Name, Month and Year in the appropriate Client Information spaces on the (12) *Quick & Simple Monthly Itemized Report Forms.*

5.      Put the (12) *Quick & Simple Monthly Itemized Report Forms* into a file jacket and write

*Monthly Report Forms* on the top edge of the file jacket.

6.    Place the file jacket into the Expense Receipt File Box.

7.    Take another file jacket and mark the top edge with *Per Diem Lodging & Meal Logs.* Put the (12) *Per Diem Lodging & Meal Log* forms into the file jacket. Place the file jacket into the Expense Receipt File Box.

8.    The final set-up step is to take another file jacket and write *Monthly Uncategorized Expense Forms* on the top edge of the jacket. Put your *Monthly Uncategorized Expense* Forms in the jacket. Place the file jacket into the Expense Receipt File Box.

# CHAPTER THREE

# QUICK AND SIMPLE RECORD KEEPING SYSTEM

# INSTRUCTIONS

1.     All expense receipts that you collect through the course of your business day should be placed in the expanding wallet each time you get into your truck. This is your central expense receipt collection point. By accumulating all of your receipts in one location you are far less likely to misplace or lose any receipts. As an Owner/ Operator, each $100 in unrecorded expense receipts will cost you over $40 in taxes.

REMEMBER: *a lost or misplaced receipt is like throwing cash in the trash!!*

2.     On the first of each month take one of the *Monthly Itemized Report* forms from its file jacket. Fill in all the information at the top of the form. On the bottom left side of the form write down your beginning odometer mileage for the month. Now put this form back into its file jacket. You won't need this form again until the end of the month.

3.     At the beginning of each month take one of the *Quick & Simple Per Diem Lodging and Meals Log* forms from its file jacket. Fill in the appropriate Client Information along with the correct month and year. Attach this form to the front of your driver's log book. At the completion of each day, you write the city, county, and state of the location you took your longest break or where you slept the longest. Write in the appropriate box

where you slept: home, sleeper, or other place. The Meals and Lodging columns are where you list your per diem amount for Meals and Lodging the end of each day. (Refer to **Chapter Five**, *Category 14 Meals per Diem* for instructions on how to figure your per diem rates for this form.)

4.      At the end of each day remove all your receipts from the expanding wallet and separate them according to expense category. Those are the 30 expense categories you have on each of the *Standard Expense Category Tracker Forms* glued to the front of the   file jackets.

**NOTE:** *The best way to become familiar with each expense category and its corresponding code # is to make an extra copy of the Monthly Itemized Report form and glue it to the front of your file jacket that contains the same form. Or there is a List of the Thirty Most Common Trucker's Deductions on page **85** of this book. You can pull it out and refer to it as you look at each receipt to determine its correct Standard Expense Category.*

5.      Take a highlighter pen and write the corresponding Standard Expense Category Number on the receipt. At the same time also *CIRCLE* the total on the receipt.

**IMPORTANT:** *DON'T HIGHLIGHT YOUR RECEIPT TOTALS AS THE HIGHLIGHTER INK WILL CAUSE THE INK ON THE RECEIPT TO DISAPPEAR.*

6.      If you are not sure in which Standard Expense Category the receipt belongs, take one of the *Quick & Simple Monthly Uncategorized Expense* forms. Write your name and month in the appropriate areas on the top of the form in the spaces. Next list the item purchased and the amount paid in the correct columns. Place the receipt in the file jacket containing the Monthly Uncategorized Expense forms. Send the form to your accountant or bookkeeper; he will be able to determine the proper expense category for that particular purchase. (You may also refer to **Chapter 5**, *Record keeping for the Owner/Operator, page 3,* to determine the criteria for a deductible expense.)

       **REMEMBER:** *If you're not sure the purchased item is an expense, don't lose your 40.5 cents per dollar of potential savings by not having it checked out and properly categorized.*

Once you receive the Correct Category and Code Number from your accountant or bookkeeper, remove the questioned receipt from the *Uncategorized Monthly Expense* form file jacket and place it in the appropriate *Expense Category*

*Tracker* file jacket. Once you have the questioned receipt properly filed and categorized, follow the steps in Step 6 & 7 below.

7.     Take each receipt and make sure it has its Expense Category Number written on it and the total on the receipt circled with the highlighter pen. Separate the receipts by number. Now place each receipt in its appropriate *Expense Category Tracker* file jacket.

8.     At the end of every week, remove the receipts from each *Quick & Simple Expense Category Tracker* file jacket and add all the totals you circled on each receipt for that Expense Category only.  (Be sure and remove only one Expense Category's receipts from a file jacket at a time so receipts from different expense categories can't get mixed up.) Take the total from each Expense Category's receipts and write the total in the corresponding month and week slot on the *Quick & Simple Expense Category Tracker* forms attached to the front of each *Quick & Simple Expense Category Tracker* file jacket.

**Example:** *You spent $21.00 on ComChek™ transaction fees the second week of March.  This would go into Banking Fees Code # 1. Find March in the far left column; find the Second Week Total in the columns to the right. Here's where you'd write $21.00*

9.    Take each set of totaled receipts and put them in a # 10 mailing envelope; and write the category name and number, the month and year on the front of the envelope. Place this envelope back into its corresponding *Expense Category Tracker* file jacket for its permanent filing location

10.    At the end of each month, take each of your *Category Expense Tracker* forms; add the weekly totals together and write this amount in the monthly total column for that particular month.

11.    At the end of each month, remove the *Monthly Itemized Report* form you started at the beginning of the month from its file jacket in the *Expense Receipt File Box*. Next go through each *Expense Category Tracker* form for each category and put the current month's total from each category in the corresponding Expense Category Space on the *Monthly Itemized Report* form. You now complete your *Monthly Itemized Report* form by writing your "End of Month" odometer mileage reading in the bottom right corner.

12.                          You are now ready to mail, fax, or scan the *Monthly Itemized Report* form, the *Uncategorized Expense* form, *Per Diem Lodging and Meals Log* form, your *settlement statements,* and a copy of your *Trucking Business Checking Account register* to your accountant, bookkeeper or CPA. Or you may elect to enter the totals into your own accounting program. If you

are the do-it-yourself type, refer to **Chapter Five** Record keeping for the Owner/Operator. Or you may contact Esta Klatzkin, EA, www.knowtaxes.com (818-345-7456; 10-6 PST) or John Turner,CPA at www.truckersaccountant.com (866-442-6657; 9-5 CST) for more information about their services.

# REMEMBER:

*Every dollar of each and every business expense receipt is worth 40 ½ cents in your pocket. But, you must have a copy of each receipt to get the deduction to keep that money in your pocket.*

# CHAPTER FOUR

# QUICK & SIMPLE RECORD KEEPING SYSTEM

# WHAT TO DO WHEN THERE ARE NO RECEIPTS

There are times when getting a receipt for a business expense is just not possible.
Examples:

- Pay phone call
- Exact change toll
- Tips or gratuities
- Business equipment purchases at flea markets or yard sales

It is best to make every attempt to get a receipt each time you make a business purchase. But when all efforts come back without that slip of paper showing a record of your purchase, the IRS permits you to keep an expense log. To have your expense log allowed in an audit it must contain the following information:

## Quick & Simple Expense Log

### 4 PROFITS EXPENSE LOG

| Month: _____ , 2 _____ | | | | Clients Name_____ Account #_____ | | | |
|---|---|---|---|---|---|---|---|
| Date: | Category # | Amount | Purchased from.... | Address | City, | | State |
| | | | | | | | |
| | | | | | | | |
| | | | | | | | |
| | | | | | | | |
| | | | | | | | |
| | | | | | | | |
| | | | | | | | |
| | | | | | | | |
| | | | | | | | |
| | | | | | | | |
| | | | | | | | |
| | | | | | | | |

The log must be kept in a day by day or chronological style. You must substantiate each individual expense.

The log must be kept in a day-by -day or chronological style. You must substantiate each individual expense as to:

- Amount
- Time & Date
- Place (Business Name, Address, City and State)
- Item or Service purchased
- Business Purpose
- If entertainment, it must also include:
  Person or Persons Entertained.
  Their business relationship to you.

This form is included in your *Quick & Simple Record Keeping Forms* available for download at www.truckersbookstore.com. Go to the end of **Chapter One** for instructions on how to obtain your *Quick & Simple Record Keeping Forms*.

# CHAPTER FIVE


# QUICK & SIMPLE RECORD KEEPING SYSTEM

# RECORD KEEPING FOR OWNER/OPERATORS

The first step in reducing taxes is to learn what is deductible. A deductible business expense is defined as "an ordinary and necessary expense you incur while furthering your trade, profession, or activity for profit."

## Ordinary and Necessary Business Expenses

An ordinary expense is one that is common and accepted in your business, trade, or profession. The courts have also interpreted this to mean customary, usual, or normal. A necessary expense is one that is helpful and appropriate for your trade, business, or profession. However, an expense does not have to be indispensable to be considered necessary.

## Reasonable

Although deductions are given to businesses as incentives for starting and staying in business, they are not meant to be abused. There must always be a degree of reasonableness.

## Combined Business and Personal Expenses

If you incur an expense for something that is partly for business and partly personal, you must separate the business portion from the personal benefit. You may deduct only the part that is for business. This guideline applies to tangible property like computers, cars, etc., not for events like meals, travel, and recreation.

☞**EXAMPLE**: *If you took out a loan and used 70% of the money for your business and the other 30% for a family vacation, you may deduct as a business expense only 70% of the interest you pay on the loan. Or, if you use a computer 95% for business and 5% for personal use, you can deduct 95% of computer-related expenses.*

**Record Keeping Note:** *Should you have expenses that don't seem to fit into the following categories, categorize them as you wish and assign business codes from Number 31 onward.*

## How Much Can Be Deducted?
The IRS has said that "You cannot deduct more for a business expense than the amount you actually spend. **There is usually no other limit on how much you can deduct, provided that the amount is reasonable.**" (IRS pub. 535, Nov. 89)

## The 30 Most Common Business Deductions

✎**TIP**: *Familiarizing yourself with these deductions is the most important exercise you can do! Read this section over and over again. The most important thing is to learn: what is deductible, not necessarily which category an expense falls into. Many people develop needless anxiety over how to classify an expense. Don't* *worry; a lot of expenses overlap, and even the IRS doesn't have a crystal-clear understanding of each category. Just concentrate on learning what's deductible and how to structure expenses, and if you categorize an expense incorrectly, your tax preparer will probably catch it at the time of filing anyway.*

## 1. Banking Fees

*Fees and charges, including check printing, automatic teller charges, overdraft protection, theft protection costs, stop payment fees, penalties and late fees from your business bank accounts and credit cards.*

The IRS prefers that you have a bank account and charge cards in the business name, but they do not require you to have them. This is highly recommended for corporations and may be mandatory under certain state laws. Check with the local authorities. You may use your personal bank account and credit cards for business use (although not recommended), but you should always distinguish personal from business expenses, deposits, and transfers.

☞**EXAMPLE**: *You used your credit card 100 times during the year, and 68 of the charges on the card were business-related. You are entitled to deduct the actual expenses, as well as a corresponding 68% of your annual membership* *fees. A corresponding percentage of interest generated from your business charges can be fully deductible on your business return, but no personal interest deduction is allowable.*

Although not an IRS requirement, it is recommended after the business start-up period that you put your company's bank account and charge cards in the company name.

*✎TIP: When opening up a checking account for your business, preferably at a business bank and not an S&L, be sure to have your cancelled checks returned to you with your statement. Request a month-end statement for ease of reconciliation. The IRS frowns on checking accounts that use carbon copies from a check register and may not even accept the duplicates in an audit situation. Should you be audited, the IRS may insist upon seeing the original checks, copies on microfiche, or electronic images from your bank. At the time of this writing, microfiche copies of checks average $1.00 per check in most states.*

## 2. Business Gifts

*You may give away gifts to as many customers, associates, or prospective customers or associates as you deem appropriate, but you are limited to only one gift per person per year. The value of the gift may not exceed $25. (If the gift cost $40, you can only write off $25.)*

Acceptable reasons for giving gifts are:
- • To promote your business's goodwill
- • For referrals
- • To reward employees or associates for performance
- • To improve cooperation

Deductible gifts do not have to be related to your company's product or service.
You may find that in many situations, a gift may also be viewed as an entertainment expense. Since entertainment expenses have a 50% deductible limitation and business gifts the $25 limitation, depending on the cost of the expense, you may elect either category – except when the gift is prepackaged food or beverage intended for future consumption.

☞**EXAMPLE:** *A ticket to a sporting event given to a customer can be treated as a gift, but if you attend the event with the customer, it must then be written off as entertainment.*

If your business is organized as a partnership, the partnership can only give one gift annually to each client, associate, or prospective client or associate. Each partner cannot give a gift to a client, associate, or prospective client or associate. If the recipient of a business gift is organized as a partnership, you cannot give a gift to each partner and deduct more than one gift.

The documentation required for business gifts is subject to the same rules governing entertainment deductions: who, what, when, where, and why. When purchasing a gift, it is always wise to write the name of the recipient on the receipt. If you do not have a receipt, then the recipient's name, business purpose and amount of the gift should be written in your daily journal.

## 3. Claims

*Property damage claims and freight damage claims.*

There are two different types of claims paid out by the Owner/Operator:

1. Property damage claims:  These claims involve damage done to a fixed property. The property has been damaged in some manner by the Owner/Operator. Damage may be to the walls, floors, doors, steps, carpet or landscaping on a piece of property. This property does not necessarily belong to the shipper or the receiver.

2. Freight damage claims:  Any damage done to an item that is going to be shipped, or is in the process of being shipped and is in the care, custody and control of the Owner/Operator is a freight damage claim. You are responsible for the item until it is released to either the shipper or the receiver.

Expense costs are incurred by the Owner/Operator in both situations. There are two methods used in handling claims. The carrier (trucking company) may pay the claim and then debit the Owner/Operator's account for the costs, or the Owner/Operator can pay the owner(s) of the damaged property directly.

Deductibles usually vary according to the individual Owner/Operator's claims liability factor or percentage. This is based on dollars paid in claims on behalf of the Owner/Operator, and the dollars of the line haul he has been paid over a nine-month period. The deductible on Freight Claims ranges from a high of $1,000 to a low of $0. On property Damage Claims, there is a flat rate deductible per claim charged to the Owner/Operator.

In some cases, the Owner/Operator may opt to pay a small claim directly to the damaged party. This will hasten settlement for the shipper or receiver and avoid having a charge put on the Owner/Operator's claim expense ratio. An adjustment to this ratio may either increase the Owner/Operator's deductible or reduce it. All deductibles that are charged to the Owner/Operator by the trucking company the Owner/Operator is contracted to, would appear on the monthly statement.

If a claim is paid directly to the damaged party, the Owner/Operator needs to get a receipt signed by both the receiving party and the Owner/Operator. It must include the shipper's name, address, order number, inventory number, and name of item, description of damage, date of original purchase, original cost, replacement cost, and agreed-upon settlement amount. It is a good idea to pay with a business check to complete the paper trail. The receipt and copy of the check should be kept for a claims expense deduction.

Items purchased to replace items lost or destroyed in handling or transport of the shipment, prior to or at the time of delivery, would also be reported in this category. Receipts for items purchased to be used to repair damaged items would be categorized as either "Tools" or "Truck Supplies." They are not reported as a Claims expense.

✎**TIP:** *Remember to keep all receipts!*

## 4. Communication

*All telephone costs including installation and monthly fees, service charges for call waiting, conference calling, speed dialing, call forwarding, etc;, message units, long distance charges, cellular phones, beepers, pagers, voice mail, answering machines or payment for taking phone messages, facsimile machines, internet fees, and uses of pay phones or calling cards.*

If you have a business, it is not necessary to have both a personal and business telephone in order to deduct business telephone costs, although it is recommended. If you use only one telephone line for both business and personal calls, the calls allocable to the business are deductible. You will need to keep track of them.

The installation fees of the first telephone line that enables an individual to obtain local phone service is not deductible, even if that line is to be used partially for business. However, the actual business calls on that line are deductible in full.

In situations where a person maintains an office outside the home and also uses his or her home telephone for business calls, it is more difficult to deduct home telephone expenses unless it can be shown that the nature of the business requires scheduling or other business discussions outside of normal business hours.

✎**TIP:** *In order to simplify deducting expenses for a home telephone whether or not you have an office outside of the home, it is advisable to have your home business telephone number printed on your business card. Expenses for cash payments to pay phones are deductible if they are documented in your daily journal. Business calls from a cellular phone, mobile or installed in a vehicle, are* *deductible, but the actual phone may have to be depreciated.*

✏**TIP:** *It is advisable to have a separate business telephone line. You can deduct the complete telephone bill, cost of installation, and the cost of the instrument.*
*If you have voice mail or an answering service that you use for both the business and the home, you can only deduct the business percentage (use the same percentage as the percent of the telephone bill allocable for business). The same percentage applies in calculating the deductible percentage of an answering machine and message tapes. Most answering machines, if less than $200, can be "expensed" rather than depreciated.*

If you purchase a "call forwarding" service from your local phone company in order to use an answering service, these costs are deductible. If you purchase a multi-line telephone, so you can forward your business line and still be able to use another line for personal calls, then a percentage of the actual telephone may be deducted or depreciated.

☞**EXAMPLE:** *You purchase a 3-line telephone and two of the lines are dedicated to business; therefore, 2/3 of the cost of the phone is deductible (and of course the installation and monthly fee of the two business lines are fully deductible).*

# 5. Dues & Subscriptions

*Newspaper and magazine subscriptions and purchases from newsstands. Membership, association, and organizational dues to associations, societies, and organizations that provide business education, trade information and/or support, referrals, or forums to present your business.*

Dues are deductible when membership privileges are used to advance the business interests of the individual. Sometimes the "business interests" of the individual may be general enough to include business networking. Country club and health club dues are **not deductible**. Publications that directly relate to your business are fully deductible. However, like educational expenses that do not directly relate to your business, publications that provide information and advice helpful to your business may be deductible.

☞**EXAMPLE**: *Publications purchased that have your competitor's ads may be deductible if you are conducting market research on their effectiveness; purchasing a non-business-related publication that contains an article/story or data that pertains to your business; or purchasing a publication that you would like to review in order to determine whether or not you would like to advertise in it.*

*✎**TIP***: *It may be advantageous to have all subscriptions or periodicals taken out in the business name and sent to the business address even if the address is your home office address.*

## 6. Entertainment

*Costs of meals, theatre, shows, concerts, games, amusement parks, galleries, sporting events, ski trips, etc., while promoting your business with clients, associates, and prospective clients and associates. All of these are always only 50% deductible. Business meals for transportation employees are 70% deductible for 2004 and 2005.*

An entertainment deduction is only allowed if the taxpayer establishes that the expenditure is directly related to the active conduct of the taxpayer's trade or business; and that business must be discussed directly before, during, or after the expenditure. An expenditure is deemed to be directly related to an individual's trade or business if it meets all four of the following criteria:

1.    At the time of the expenditure, the individual must have more than a general expectation of deriving income or a business benefit other than goodwill at some indefinite future time.

2.    During the entertainment period, the individual is actually engaged in a

business meeting, negotiation, discussion, or other bona fide transaction other than entertainment for the purpose of obtaining a business benefit.

3.  The principle character of the expenditure must be the active conduct of the individual's trade or business. It is not necessary that more time be devoted to business than to entertainment to meet this requirement.

4.  The expenditure is allocable to the individual and a person or persons with whom he or she engages in the active conduct or trade or business during the entertainment or with whom he or she would be so engaged if it were not for circumstances beyond the individuals' control.

It is not mandatory that income or a tangible business benefit be derived from every entertainment expense in order to be deductible.

"Goodwill entertainment" is a form of entertainment (still only 50% deductible) in which business is not discussed during the entertainment, but on the condition that business had been or will be discussed **directly before or after** the entertainment. When entertaining, the IRS prefers the expenditure be in a "clear business setting" where there are not significant distractions.

Under certain circumstances, the IRS may take the position that in order for a taxpayer to deduct his or her meal while entertaining (when not away from home overnight), he or she may have to prove that the cost of the meal exceeded what would have been spent had the individual been alone in a non-business environment. This rule is usually only invoked when the IRS feels the entertainment costs are "abusive."

☞**Secret:** *To help reduce the chance that your entertainment will be perceived as "abusive," it is recommended to keep your non-deductible entertainment receipts as well as deductible ones, so in the event of an audit you can demonstrate that you didn't write off all, or a majority of your entertainment. This technique enables you to look fair and reasonable.*

Meals and entertainment expenses incurred on behalf of business associates, assistants, partners, and spouses with a business relationship have been allowed. In these situations, if there are many such meals or entertaining, especially with the same person, the IRS may feel they are "abusive" and limit the deduction.

It is always best to have in addition to a receipt of a meal, contemporary records (calendar or diary entries) of the expenditure, detailing cost, date, place, business purpose, business relationship, and business benefit expected. There are permissible exceptions: when a person's records are lost, stolen, or destroyed because of circumstances beyond his control like fire, flood, earthquake, etc. If necessary, in audit, documentation can always be enhanced by oral and written testimony and corroborative evidence.

The IRS may try to disallow some or all entertainment expenses if they deem them to be lavish or extravagant. Expenses cannot be disallowed because they are above a fixed dollar amount or occur at high profile establishments. They must be "reasonable" and consider all the facts and circumstances. Moreover, "While the law does not impose upon the business person the duty of entertaining in the cheapest possible manner, the choice of highly expensive modes of achieving an alleged business objective is relevant when the issue of whether business or personal motives were involved. There was no showing that the taxpayer realistically anticipated that profits would repay the cost of such entertainment or indeed that they ever did." (T. C. Memo, 1979-291)

📁**Secret:** *The best form of advertising is word of mouth – with your mouth full of tax-deductible food!*

# 7. Equipment – New Purchase

*Office furniture and equipment, computers and accessories, tools, copying machines, facsimiles, telephone systems, cellular phones, vehicles, etc.*

Many items over $200 in value may not be 100% deductible in the year you purchase them, but rather a percentage of the item may be deductible over a period of years. Depreciation is an economic concept that says when you place equipment/property into service for the production of business income, because of the subsequent wear and tear on it, that equipment over time is losing its value. The cost of that loss of value becomes a tax deduction known as depreciation.

Property is depreciable if it meets these IRS requirements:
1. It must be used in business or held for the production of income.
2. It must have a determinable life, and that life must be longer than one year.
3. It must be something that wears out, decays, gets used up, becomes obsolete, or loses value from natural causes.

Depreciable property may be tangible or intangible. Tangible property is any property that can be seen or touched. Intangible property includes copyrights or franchise fees. Depreciable property may be real or personal. Personal property is machinery and equipment that is not real estate. Real property is land and anything erected on, growing on, or attached to land. Land itself is never depreciable.

You must also depreciate property that is placed in service but is temporarily idle. For example, you may have purchased a truck or van intending to make large deliveries of product, but it was never used during the year – it must still be depreciated. The rule is allowed or allowable (use it or lose it).

It is important to note that for equipment to be depreciated, it does not have to be equipment purchased after you started your business. In many start-up situations in small businesses, people often begin using equipment that was once personal in nature; i.e., home computer, telephone answering machine, desk, etc. This type of conversion of personal to business use is officially called "placed assets in business service," and the equipment termed "equipment on hand."

✒**TIP:** *Go through your home and make a list of all items over $200 in value that you have placed in service for business use. Include the description of the equipment, the date it was placed in service, the percentage it is used for business, and the fair market value of the item. It is not necessary to have the original receipts for the items being* *placed in service since you will be depreciating the item based on the value of the item at the time it was placed in service, not when originally purchased. Equipment on hand depreciation must use the straight line method of depreciation.*

*The IRS has assigned all equipment a useful life. A useful life is that period of time during which the IRS feels the equipment will be "useful" without major repair or complete malfunctioning. Most items are assigned a useful life of 3, 5, or 7 years.*

✐✐**IMPORTANT TIP:** *A special and little-known way of "accelerating" depreciation deductions is called* **Section 179**. *This is an IRS provision that allows a small business person to "expense out" (deduct 100%) up to $102,000 worth of business equipment or property in 2004, and $105,000 in 2005, as opposed to deducting only a portion over time using conventional depreciation methods. For electing* **Section 179**, *these are the guidelines:*

- President Bush signed into law a $350 billion tax cut bill that includes several items targeted to the small-business community. For tax years 2003-2005, the "Section 179" small-business deduction limit for equipment purchases increases to $100,000 (from $25,000).

48

- Additionally, the bill provides an additional first-year depreciation deduction equal to 50 percent of the adjusted basis of qualified property (rather than 30 percent under current law). The property must be acquired after May 5, 2003, and before Jan. 1, 2005. The law also includes dividends and capital gains tax cuts for individuals, accelerated income-tax relief, marriage penalty relief and more.

1. Typically, if property for business has a useful life of more than one year, the cost must be spread across several tax years as depreciation with a portion of the cost deducted each year.

2. But there is a way to immediately receive these income tax benefits in one tax year. The provisions of Internal Revenue Code Section 179 allow a sole proprietor, partnership or corporation to fully expense tangible property in the year it is purchased.

3. And in 2003, tax-law changes made this option much more appealing by dramatically increasing – from $25,000 to $100,000 – the amount that can be written off immediately.

## 8. Equipment Rental

*U-Haul, shuttle truck, tractor, lift, computer, etc.*

Keep all rental agreements and contracts as well as receipts for all equipment rented or leased. They are fully deductible at time of payment.

## 9. Insurance (Non-Health)

*Liability, indemnification, merchandise and inventory, overhead, and credit insurance on policies covering potential losses from debt nonpayment, employees group medical, dental, and legal plans, and worker's compensation. Fire, theft, property, flood, mortgage, and casualty insurance on property outside of the home.*

In addition to the above, certain types of bond payments that must be issued by law, or contractual obligation in order to ensure the company's performance and compliance in a business venture, can be deductible.

## 10. Interest

*Interest on business loans, credit cards used for business; and installment payments on auto, furnishings, and equipment, placed in business service.*

As of 1991, consumer interest is no longer deductible (except for interest on mortgage and home equity loans), but interest on the purchases of business-related items is fully deductible. The deductible amount of interest is allocable to the business use of an item.

☞**EXAMPLE:** *If you use your computer 78% for business, then only 78% of the computer loan interest is deductible on your return.*

The IRS has stated that "It is not necessary for the parties to a transaction to label a payment made for the use of money as interest for it to be so treated. The facts of a transaction control its character, not the terminology." One tax court further ruled that "A taxpayer's obligation may constitute genuine indebtedness even where the underlying transactions are without substance, so long as the obligor is bound under traditional commercial law concepts."

For an interest expense to be deductible, it does not have to be specifically termed "interest" in a contractual or oral agreement but rather be a "reasonable" obligation for indebtedness. In some situations, state usury laws place limits on how much interest a business can charge, so to comply with the law and still receive a higher percentage on loans, or products or services that are on installment, the following premium charges may be charged instead: late fees, hazard charges, acquisition charges, loan processing fees or points, and premium charges might be charged instead. Interest is deductible regardless of what it has been termed in order to avoid state usury laws. Likewise, prepayment charges are deductible because they represent an increased fee for borrowing money for a shorter period of time. It is not a requirement that the lender have the interest charges reflect a "constant" percentage of the lump sum financed. A deduction was given for payments on borrowed money where both lender and borrower had agreed that the size of the payments would be contingent on the size and frequency of payments.

☞**EXAMPLE:** *One might make a loan and set a different rate for weekly payments, another for bimonthly payments, yet another on monthly payments in excess of a specified amount; i.e., $25 fee for weekly payments, $75 fee for bimonthly payments, and a $50 fee for monthly payments in excess of $1,000.*

Certain restrictions apply to interest on insurance policy loans used for business; the interest deduction is only allowable for loans up to $50,000, and only a partial deduction for loans exceeding $50,000.

# 11. Labor

*Payment to day laborers and other independent contractors.*

The independent contract laborer is paid upon the completion of services performed. He or she is paid per weight, day or hour and will provide all necessary equipment required to do the job. The services to be performed will be enumerated at time of hire.

A contractual labor agreement should be drawn up each time an independent contractor's service is needed. It should contain:

1. Laborer is over age 18.

2. Contractor understands the terms of the agreement.

3. He or she is responsible for all of their own tax obligations, fees, licenses, insurance, etc.

4. No benefits are available to the laborer.

5. Contractor's services are offered to other companies and the general public.

6. Laborer will provide his/her own equipment, tools, transportation and meals.

A Form W-9 should be completed and signed by the independent contract laborer. It contains the name, address, Social Security number and signature of the worker. At year-end, a 1099 Form should be filed if the recipient received $600 or more in annual compensation. These forms are easy to fill out and may be obtained from the IRS or a local stationery store. (See "Professional Fees" for filing instructions and due date.)

Remember, compensation should always be reasonable and a deduction is more likely to be allowed when a 1099 Form is filed. Although the IRS, as well as state agencies, would like to have the name and identification number (Social Security or Federal ID number) of hired help, there are some situations where it is common for temporary help not to provide their true names or identification numbers and to insist on cash payment. These types of payments were deductible to an Owner/Operator using individuals to load and unload his vehicles even though the hired help didn't furnish identification. In its decision, the court noted that the Owner/Operator did not create these circumstances.

## 12. Lodging Per Diem

A taxpayer must substantiate the amount, time, place, and business purpose of expenses paid or incurred in traveling away from home. Although the taxpayer has the option of keeping the actual records of travel expenses, the IRS has provided per diem allowances under which the amount of away from home meals and lodging expenses may be deemed to be substantiated. These per diem allowances eliminate the need for substantiating actual costs (Rev. Proc. 04-60). Per Diem allowances may be used only if the time, place and business purpose of the travel are substantiated by adequate records or other evidence.

Lodging receipts are not required if per diem allowances are used to substantiate such expenses. The locality of travel is where the taxpayer who is traveling on business away from home stops for sleep or rest.

The federal per diem rate for lodging depends upon the locality of travel. For various geographic areas within the continental United States (the 48 contiguous states plus the District of Columbia), the federal per diem rates have been established by locality. The CONUS (Continental United States) Table is equal to the sum of a maximum lodging amount for that locality. Call your local IRS office for the current per diem rate list. And consult a tax professional for any other changes.

In lieu of using the maximum per diem rate from the CONUS Table, the high-low method, which is a simplified method for determining lodging per diem, can be used to compute per diem allowances for travel within the continental United States. This method divides all CONUS localities into two categories: high-cost or low-cost localities.

☞**NOTE**: *Federal per diem rate method. New CONUS per diem rates become effective on October 1 of each year, and remain in effect through September 30 of the following year. Drivers using the per diem rate method during the first 9 months of a year January 1 – September 30 must continue under the same method through the end of that calendar year (December 31). However, for travel by these drivers from October 1 through December 31, they may choose to continue using the same per diem rates or use the new rates. Just as the High-Low method, the driver must continue using the same method for the entire calendar year. In 2004, the high-cost was $161 and the low-cost was $90 for per diem lodging expenses. In 2005, the high-cost is $153 and the low-cost is $91 for lodging per diem.*

## 13. Maintenance & Repair (Non-Vehicle)

*Cleaning carpet, furniture, insect extermination, etc. Interior and exterior decorating items used at your NON-HOME office – paintings, potted plants, seasonal decorations, etc.*

Minor repairs, painting, flooring and resurfacing that may not be construed as capital improvements are deductible, as well as small tools and equipment used in such repairs and maintenance. These items with the proper receipts may be classified as either "Tools" or "Truck Supplies."

## 14. Meals Per Diem

Meals and incidental expense per diem allowances may be used to substantiate the taxpayer's expenses. If M&IE (Meals and Incidental Expenses) are substantiated using a per diem allowance, the entire amount is treated as a food and beverage expense subject to the 50% limitation on meal and entertainment expenses. The M&IE rate must be prorated for partial days of travel away from home. A truck driver who meets all of the requirements listed below will be able to take 75% of the M&IE rate for meals, instead of 50% allowed other self-employed individuals. The self-employed person must actually prove, through adequate records, or sufficient corroborative evidence, the time, place, and business purpose of the travel (Rev. Proc. 04-60). For the transportation industry, in 2004 an M&IE rate of $41 for CONUS travel and $45 for OCONUS travel (Outside Continental United States) may be used by self-employed persons. For 2005 M&IE rate of $41 for CONUS travel and $46 for OCONUS travel (Outside Continental United States). An individual is in the transportation industry only if the individual's work:

1. Directly involves moving people or goods by airplane, barge, ship, train, or truck.
2. Regularly requires travel away from home that involves travel to localities with differing M&IE rates during a single trip.

## 15. Office Expenses

*Generally small equipment under $200 in value such as a briefcase, calculator, tape recorder, paper, pens, pencils, file folders, rulers, paper clips, paper punch, binders, stapler, staple remover, computer supplies, light bulbs, black/white boards and easels, bookkeeping and art supplies, coffee maker, cups, napkins, utensils, and guest book.*

This is really a straightforward category that does not require a great deal of elaboration. However, should you ever need a precedent for claiming supplies used in your trade, profession, or business; cite IRS Regulations Section 1.162-6.

## 16. Parking Fees

*Daily truck parking fees at truck stops, parking fees at commercial lots; as well as parking meters, when picking up supplies, tools, etc.*

Receipts are needed for all parking fees. Where receipts are unavailable, such as parking meters, annotate the cost in your diary or company log.

Indicate where parked, cost, date, and purpose; i.e., delivering shipment from Alabama to Ohio.

## 17. Permits/Licenses/Taxes

*Annual and trip permits. All licenses and regulatory fees used in connection with the business; i.e., business license, professional licenses, vehicle licenses, individual licenses, etc. Sales, excise, business portion of real estate (property), fuel, ton mile or weight distance, FHUT taxes.*

Permits issued by different states for the purpose of operating a commercial vehicle for hire within the borders of that state may be purchased in a number of different ways.

1.  A trip permit is purchased just before entering, or at the time of entering a specific state, for a predetermined period of time or miles. This may be purchased at Port of Entry, Permit Agency, such as a truck stop, or by a Permit Wire Service authorized by the specific state. The wire service is linked to the trucking company or agent/broker that holds the leasing agreement or contract of that Owner/Operator. All methods of purchase of a trip permit are determined by the issuing state.

2.  An annual permit is acquired for a specific fiscal year as determined by the issuing

state. In today's licensing environment, most states belong to I.F.T.A. (International Fuel Taxing Authority), an international organization of United States, Canadian, and Mexican state fuel taxation departments. These states have banded together for the purpose of issuing a single permit for the collection of state (not federal) fuel taxes. This single I.F.T.A. permit is purchased at the same time as the "base plate" license and is provided by the state of registration (issuer of the base plate). There are a few other states that issue annual permits such as Oregon. These are obtained per the regulations and laws of the issuing state.

Recording of permit purchases will occur through two different sources:
1. Agency statement debit (deduction) either at the time of issue or by other means as determined by the Owner/Operator's agency contract.

2. Actual purchase of permit paid directly to the state or issuing broker by the Owner/Operator.

Generally, permits issued by a governmental authority that are not renewable are not deductible because the benefits usually last more than one year; but may be amortized. The costs of permits that have to be renewed periodically are deductible.

There are three different types of licenses:
1. Vehicle licenses are required by state law or regulation. They are used in the operation of your business. Licenses are needed for both primary, support and service vehicles such as semi-tractors, trucks and trailers.

2. There are many types of individual licenses required by state law or regulation. They include CDL (Commercial Drivers License), Fork Lift Operators license, Heavy Equipment license, etc.

3. A business license may be required by the county or city where you conduct business. The requirement varies from state to state.

Taxes charged to a business are deductible if they are directly connected with the trade or business. The deduction is allowed only for the year in which the taxes are paid or accrued: Code Sec 164(a). Some of the taxes paid by the trucking industry are:
1. Excise and Sales tax is charged when purchasing tires, certain machinery and equipment. A federal excise tax of 12% is assessed on trailer chassis or body, parts and accessories installed on taxable vehicles within 6 months after being

placed in service. If you have an ICC or DOT number there will be no sales tax charged.

2. Real Estate (Property) tax is assessed on the value of the property by the taxing authority. This tax is deductible if the real estate is used in the course of your business. It may be necessary to allocate the percentage of business use and apply that percentage accordingly.

3. Personal Property tax is owed on the value of tangible personal property used in the business such as furniture and fixtures, machinery, equipment and supplies. It is usually taxed by the state. In some parts of the country, it may be required to be paid by a county or city.

4. Fuel and Ton Mile Taxes are levied on commercial interstate vehicles. They are based on the number of miles traveled by the permitted vehicle in the state where the tax is charged.

   a. Fuel Tax: Every time you purchase fuel in most states, they collect the fuel tax at the pump. As long as you turn in the original copy of the fuel receipt with your logs, your account with that state will be credited for the

amount of the tax. Most states tax at a
rate equal to 5 miles to a gallon.

☞**EXAMPLE**: *You travel 200 miles in a state that
charges 20 cents tax per gallon of fuel. They will
charge $8.00 tax for traveling through the state. If
you purchase 40 gallons of fuel in that state and
turn in your receipts for credit, you owe no
additional tax. (40 x .20 = $8.00) If you didn't
purchase any fuel while traveling through that
state, you would be charged the $8.00 tax (usually
debited to your statement by the agency that holds
your contract). If you purchased fuel and did not
turn in the receipt, your statement would be
debited, and you just allowed yourself to be taxed
twice.*

    b. Ton Mile or Weight Distance Tax:
This tax is based on your apportioned
weight on your "base plate"
registration, the permit issued by the
levying state, and the miles traveled
through the state. Every state tax is
different. This charge is usually
debited from your statement
regardless of fuel receipts.

    5. FHUT (Federal Highway Use Tax): this
annual tax is charged by the U.S.
government in mid-summer. Normally,
the van line, agency, or trucking

company you are contracted to will debit your statement for this fee.

You need not separate taxes paid on actual purchases for business use if you include them with the purchase price of the item you are deducting as an expense.

## 18. Postage & Shipping

*Postage, whether stamps or metered mail, for all business correspondence including letters, bills, notices and holiday cards, as well as all costs relating to certified, registered, and insured business mailings. Parcel post shipments, handling charges, and special carrier services like UPS, DHL, Fed Ex, etc.*

If you send a card (Christmas, birthday, or anniversary) to someone who has a business relationship to you, the cost of the card and postage is deductible even if you do not sign it in your business name or make reference to your business. It is advisable to make some reference to your business unless it would appear too commercial or "pushy."

✎**TIP:** *One way to deduct most of your postage, even for semi-personal correspondence and bill payments, is to convert those into business direct mail opportunities by enclosing your business card. A client who enclosed his business card* *along with his home electric utility payment subsequently received a call from a clerk working for the utility company who scheduled a move with his agency!*

## 19. Professional Fees

*Payment and compensation for independently contracted business related services including, but not limited to, messenger services, attorneys, accountants, consultants and day laborers.*

Payments must be for business related services. So, if you use a consultant who also performs services that could be construed as non-business related, it is recommended a copy be kept of the invoice or contract specifying the business nature of the services performed.

Compensation should always be reasonable. In determining reasonableness, the IRS will look at factors like the nature of the work, time spent, competitive prices, and size of the business. If the recipient of the compensation is a closely-related party (relative, lover, neighbor, etc.), this could arouse suspicion and the taxpayer must prove, in addition to the above guidelines, that the fee is commensurate with free market rates.

Deduction is more likely to be allowed when a 1099 Form is filed on the recipient. 1099s must be filed on Independently Contracted individuals or companies receiving $600 or more in annual compensation unless they are corporations. Exception: medical and legal corporations should also get 1099s.

A 1099 Form can be acquired through a local stationery store where business forms are sold, or from the IRS. The forms are easy to fill out: name, address and Social Security number or tax ID number. Each 1099 Form is designed so that the red original can be sent into the IRS and carbon copy transmittal forms sent to the recipient and in some situations to the state government as well. Keep the payer copy for your records! The original red form must be submitted to the federal government no later than the last day of February, or penalties could be incurred.

Although the IRS, as well as state agencies, would like to have the name and identification number (Social Security or Federal ID number) of hired help, there are some situations where it is common for temporary help not to provide their true names or identification numbers and to insist on cash payment. These types of payments were deductible to an Owner/Operator using individuals to load and unload his vehicles even though the hired help didn't furnish identification. In its decision, the court noted that the Owner/Operator did not create these circumstances. Of course, it is best to get as much information as possible on a Form W-9 signed by the independent contractor.

# 20. Scale Tickets/Weights

*It is the Owner/Operator's responsibility to weigh an order when necessary. Safe-Guard shipments do not require certified weight scale tickets because these shipments are moved on the basis of the "manufacturer's weight." All shipments other than those specified as manufacturer's weight must be weighed. Uncollectible transportation charges caused by noncompliance with these rules could be the sole responsibility of the Owner/Operator.*

Many trade show costs are based on the weight of the shipments. Therefore, it is mandatory to get certified weights on all shipments delivered directly to a show facility. Copies of the weight tickets must be turned in with the Bill of Lading at the time of delivery.

Weighing procedures are:

1.  Weigh each shipment.

2.  Follow company weighing rules.

3.  If your truck is overweight, report this to dispatch. Do not proceed from load site and then decide to get weights. Get weights at point of origin when you suspect an overweight. It is your responsibility and expense to go back to the load site to have the weight adjusted.

4. Place your name and identification number on the weight receipt. Turn these scale tickets in for reimbursement by your van line.

5. Overweight fines or tickets are your responsibility and will not be reimbursed.

## 21. Security

*Locks, safes, alarm systems – including installation and monitoring fees, surveillance, electronic sensors, light timers, video cameras – bodyguards, garage door openers, special lighting, polygraph tests, tear gas, mace, guard dog care and feeding, stun guns, and weapons*
.

This category is fairly straightforward, but it is worthwhile to note that Elvis Presley was reported to deduct his personal karate classes as a security deduction. Security for protection of your person is highly scrutinized by IRS unless you are a celebrity or transport substantial cash or products. It would be reasonable to incur personal security if your business required you to travel through or into high crime areas, and if without the assurances of security measures, you would not risk doing so.

## 22. Showers

*The cost of showers, incidentals such as soap, shampoo, conditioner, body lotion, wash cloths, towels, etc.*

This category is self-explanatory. Remember to get receipts for all items purchased.

## 23. Tolls

*All bridge, tunnel, road, and ferry tolls are deductible.*

You must retain a copy of each toll receipt that you pay. If you travel the same toll roads regularly, consider buying an "Easy Pass" which allows you to use these roads at a discounted rate. You must display this pass for the toll collectors to see.

## 24. Tools

*Basic tools, fire extinguisher, moving tools, dollies, hump strap, mechanical tools, filter wrench, sockets, etc.*

All business related tools and materials are deductible expenses when purchased, as long as they are required in the performance of your trade or profession. A receipt is required for proof of purchase.

## 25. Trailer Expenses

*The trailer is usually owned by the trucking company. The Owner/Operator's contract will determine his or her responsibility for maintenance and repair.*

In most cases, all repairs and maintenance are the financial responsibility of the company, agency, or van line that owns the trailer. The Owner/Operator may have to pay for repairs or maintenance at the time the work is done. Retain the receipt to be turned in at a later date for reimbursement by the company that owns the trailer. Tracking these expenses separately is necessary to insure proper reimbursement.

It is also possible that the Owner/Operator's contract may hold him or her responsible for certain expenses on the trailer due to the Owner/Operator's negligence. Some of these may be damage to the trailer from low overhang, destruction of a tire on a curb, or bottoming out and damaging the undercarriage and belly boxes. The company usually pays for items like washes, lube and greasing, worn tire replacement, road hazard tire repair, brake repair and replacement, and axle and suspension repair.

If you own the trailer you need to keep up with all repairs and maintenance expenses including washes, lube and greasing, worn tire replacement, road hazard tire repair, brake repair and replacement, and axle and suspension repair.

## 26. Travel

*Costs such as plane, helicopter, hydrofoil, train, auto, ship and bus fares. Rental cars, rental equipment, house trailer rental, meals, lodging, laundry, tips, baggage handling, and special arrangements while away from home on business.*

Business expenses while traveling are deductible if the expenditure is necessary or appropriate to the pursuit, furtherance or development of business. A trip need not be entirely dedicated to business in order to deduct some expenses. Even if the majority of time or events attended were of a personal nature, some business expenses may be deductible.

☞**EXAMPLE:** *A shoe designer was allowed expenses for travel to Italy and France where he claimed he was searching for new design ideas.*

Travel expenses are usually highly scrutinized by the IRS because of the quasi-personal benefits and potential for "abuse." Therefore, it is mandatory to maintain a daily log or journal of your activities when you travel on business. Record an item-by-item correlation of business expense, date, location, purpose, and if individual(s) are involved, the name of the individual(s) and their relationship to your business.

Although the IRS generally has very strict substantiation requirements, an IRS Revenue Agent has the flexibility to allow a reasonable amount of travel expenses without documentation if the taxpayer is able to prove the expenses with collateral evidence.

A CPA was allowed in tax court a deduction for taxicab fares even though he didn't have documentation of these expenditures. The judge reasoned/assumed that an accountant would have incurred these types of expenses in the operation of his profession.

A businessperson can deduct the cost of meals while traveling without documentation; i.e., receipts, credit card invoices, etc. He or she may choose to use a prepared IRS amount for meals, if time, place, person, and business reason can be established in a diary or similar form of record that is acceptable.

The IRS views travel expenses as those incurred while "away from home" when business responsibilities warrant overnight stay for either work, sleep, or rest. However, a person need not be away from home for at least a 24-hour period of time to be considered traveling.

In one court case, a couple driving home after attending a business conference felt that without adequate sleep and rest at a hotel they might not have returned home safely. The court allowed a deduction for the "reasonable" hotel expense.

In defining "home" when used in "traveling away from home" for tax purposes, the following factors are considered:
1. The amount of time a taxpayer spends in each location.
2. The nature of "home" and entitled to "away from home" expenses.

The three major criteria the IRS views to determine the taxpayer's "home" are:

1. Whether it has been used as lodging in the past.
2. Whether some of the living expenses are duplicated because of out-of-town lodging.
3. Whether the taxpayer continues to use the abode or has a family member living there.

Furthermore, a "home" from which a taxpayer can be away from has no geographic restrictions. It may be located in a foreign country.

Deducting expenses for one's spouse while on business is scrutinized closely because of the presumption of a personal benefit. However, a spouse's expenses on a legitimate business trip can be deductible when "it can be adequately shown that the spouse's presence on the trip had a bona fide business purpose." Regulations Section 1.162-2(c). The spouse must be either an employee of the business or a partner or corporate officer.

1. One court, in regard to business travel, went on to say that "Pleasure and business, unlike oil and water, can sometimes be mixed." degree of business activity in each place.

2. The relative portion of income earned in each location.

In order to deduct expenses "away from home," one must have a home to be away from! Individuals who continually travel; i.e., entertainers, circus and carnival help, **truckers**, etc., who are unable to show a "permanent" home other than a post office box, have been denied "away from home" expenses because "their homes were wherever they happened to be in connection with their engagements as entertainers, and the cost of their meals and lodgings were personal (nondeductible) living expenses." (T.C. Memo 1966-104)

When a person anticipates a business trip to last more than one year, there is an IRS presumption that the business travel was not temporary but rather permanent, and the taxpayer is not considered "away from home" and entitled to "away from home" expenses. The three major criteria the IRS views to determine the taxpayer's "home" are:

1. Whether it has been used as lodging in the past.

2. Whether some of the living expenses are duplicated because of out-of-town lodging.

3. Whether the taxpayer continues to use the abode or has a family member living there.

Furthermore, a "home" from which a taxpayer can be away from has no geographic restrictions. It may be located in a foreign country.

## 27. Truck/Auto Expenses

*Fuel, oil, repairs, maintenance, insurance, interest, accessories, washes and detailing, window tinting.*

You may deduct truck or automobile expenses that relate to your business. You need to implement a mileage tracking system, if using your vehicle for both business and personal use.

For a vehicle that is used exclusively for business (such as your semi-truck), you need to keep up with all repairs and maintenance expenses including washes, lube and greasing, worn tire replacement, road hazard tire repair, brake repair and replacement, axle and suspension repair, and all other maintenance or repairs completed on the vehicle. For tax proposes it works best to combine all Truck/Auto expenses into one category. For keeping track of your truck expenses for business management intentions you should set up subcategories under 27 Truck/Auto Expenses such as 27a *Accessories*, 27b *Fuel*, 27c *Preventive Maintenance*, 27d *Repairs*, 27e *Tires*, 27f *Washes*, Etc.

✎**TIP:** *When putting together your Quick and Simple Record Keeping System, list each subcategory on a separate No.10 business envelope and place in your Expense Category File Jackets as instructed in* **Chapter One**.

Should you be involved in a traffic accident resulting in a judgment, and your insurance company does not cover damages due, they may be deducted as a casualty loss. Should these "out of pocket" expenses arise from an accident occurring while pursuing your business, they can be deductible without limitation on your business return.

# 28. Truck Supplies

*Dollies, mats, rubber bands, tape, cartons, skids and pads, furniture repair kit, nuts, bolts and screws, paper, boxes, other packing materials, chains, binder, load bars, tarps, straps, etc.*

All materials and supplies necessary for your trade, business or profession are deductible with the proper documentation. This is an area where planning may increase your deductible expenses, saving you tax dollars.

# 29. Uniforms/Laundry

*Uniforms with the company name affixed on them, caps, and shoes. Costs of cleaning uniforms necessary for your business.*

In order for clothing and accessories to be considered a uniform, the uniform must be specifically required as a condition of employment and not adaptable to take the place of regular clothing. That is, the uniform should not be suitable for ordinary wear.

The IRS is very strict about being "not suitable for ordinary wear." For instance, people in the military are not allowed a deduction for the cost of their uniforms because they can be worn as everyday attire (although cleaning of the uniforms is deductible). A highway patrolman whose employer required maroon socks as part of a uniform was not allowed a deduction because he failed to prove how the socks could not be used for everyday wear. Likewise, a tennis instructor was not allowed to deduct his tennis shorts and warm-up suit.

Actual costs of uniforms which could be used for ordinary wear can be deductible if not taken home but rather kept in a locker or closet at the place of business during off hours.
Uniforms which have the name of the company affixed on them may be deductible when used solely in the course of your business, or as a form of advertising.

Since a uniform is an ordinary and necessary expense, its upkeep and maintenance is also deductible. This would include items like laundry and dry cleaning, special hangers and bags, starch, polish, waterproofing, and repair.

While traveling on business, laundry and dry cleaning costs of both uniform and ordinary wear clothing is deductible regardless of the amount of time spent traveling.

# 30. Vehicle Leases/Rentals

*Trailer, tractor, automobile, truck, etc.*

A qualified vehicle lease agreement that contains a terminal rental adjustment clause (a provision permitting or requiring the rental price to be adjusted upward or downward by reference to the amount realized by the lessor upon the sale of the vehicle) is treated as a lease for tax purposes. This provision applies only to qualified agreements with respect to a motor vehicle including a trailer. Short-term vehicle rentals, by the day, week, or month would also be deductible in this category. The lessee of a luxury car leased for business is required to include an additional amount in income to offset rental deductions for each tax year during which the car is leased. The inclusion amount is based on the cost of the car and applies to cars with a fair market value exceeding an inflation-adjusted dollar amount of $14,800 for a car with a lease term beginning in 2004. An IRS table provides the lease inclusion amount based on the fair market value dollar amount of the car and the first day of the lease term.

**Record Keeping Note:** *Should you have expenses that don't seem to fit into the preceding categories, categorize them as necessary and assign Category Codes from Number 31 onward.*

# CHAPTER SIX

## QUICK & SIMPLE RECORD KEEPING SYSTEM

## THE FINAL WORD

This book is designed for you to assemble an effective, simple, record keeping system for the lowest possible cost.

We could have purchased all the components required for the system, paid someone to assemble each individual system, warehoused the completed systems, and set up a shipping and handling department to fulfill each order. By the time we made all these arrangements, the cost of each system would be in the hundreds of dollars.

Instead, we've elected to provide you with a book of instructions on how to assemble the system; what components to purchase and where: thus saving you hundreds of dollars.

There's also an added benefit that as you purchase, download and assemble the components to the **Quick & Simple Record Keeping System for Owner/Operators** you will gain a greater understanding of the system. This will give you a shorter learning curve toward the system working at top efficiency for you.

Throughout the previous chapters, we've discussed the necessary ingredients for the **Quick & Simple Record Keeping System for Owner/Operators**.

The entire key to the usefulness and success for this system is having the correct facts, figures and data recorded and available to be sent to your accountant or entered into your bookkeeping program.

You must invest the needed amount of time gathering, recording and filing each of your receipts and costs into the correct category. Without the effort of putting the correct numbers into the system your results would be similar to not maintaining your scheduled preventive maintenance program or putting new tires on your truck but failing to inflate them. Please invest the time to gather and install the right numbers and your results will be like turning the key to a finely-tuned and maintained engine and correctly inflated tires: you will be able to run in the hammer lane to your financial destination!

# So put it in gear and join the convoy to success!

# 30 Most Common Truckers' Expense Categories List

1. BANKING FEES

2. BUSINESS GIFTS

3. CLAIMS

4. COMMUNICATIONS

5. DUES & SUBSCRIPTIONS

6. ENTERTAINMENT

7. EQUIP / NEW PURCHASE

8. EQUIP / VEHICLE RENTAL

9. INSURANCE (non-health)

10. INTEREST

11. LABOR

12. LODGING / PER DIEM

13. MAINT. / REPAIR (non-vehicle

14. MEALS / PER DIEM

15. OFFICE EXPENSES

16. PARKING FEES

17. PERMITS / LICENSES / TAXES

18. POSTAGE & SHIPPING

19. PROFESSIONAL FEES

20. SCALE TICKETS

21. SECURITY

22. SHOWERS

23. TOLLS

24. TOOLS

25. TRAILER EXPENSES

26 TRAVEL (airline bus train)

27. TRUCK / AUTO EXPENSES

28. TRUCK SUPPLIES

29. UNIFORMS / LAUNDRY

30. VEHICLE LEASES

# Authors' Biographies

## Esta Klatzkin

is a tax and financial consultant with practices in Tarzana, CA and Las Vegas, NV. She received her formal education from New York University and the New School for Social Research. Ms. Klatzkin has been Enrolled to practice before the Internal Revenue Service since 1980. She is a member of the National Association of Enrolled Agents and the California Society of Enrolled Agents. Her name is registered in Strathmore's Who's Who and Oxford's Who's Who.

She formed her first firm, Consolidated Accounting Services, in 1979 to service small and medium-sized professional practices. In 1990, she started a second practice named kNOw TAXES specializing in home-based businesses. She has been a seminar presenter for many years on various tax-saving topics.

Ms. Klatzkin thinks of herself as a small business person whose goal is to help other small business people get ahead by providing them with the tools and understanding necessary to compete in today's market place.

# Authors' Biographies

## Tim Brady

is a successful Owner/Operator recently retired from a major van line, which association had been continuous since 1981. He received his formal education from Santa Monica College; UCLA, and the University of Tennessee: Martin. The emphasis of his education was in Accounting, Marketing and Business Administration.  Mr. Brady has a successful and diversified business background, including profitable ventures in restaurant consulting and management; yacht brokerage, and fire and casualty insurance.

He is an award-winning professional truck driver; an Owner/Operator for over twenty years, and used his own Driven 4 Profits, Gearing Up 4 Profits, and Quick & Simple Record Keeping System for Owner/Operators on a daily basis. He is The Trucker's Financial Advisor on "The Open Road Café" (Sirius Trucking Network). He was interviewed for an article in Land Line (July, 2002) and has had many more articles and interviews in other major trucking publications including Transport Topics, Driver'sMag.com, Direction and The Trucker. He has a monthly financial column in Driver'sMag.com, and is a guest columnist for AMSA's Direction magazine. A local NBC-TV affiliate has repeatedly featured him in human-interest segments. He was named OverDrive Magazine's Trucker of the Month for

March 2003. On April 7, 2003, Mr. Brady received The American Moving and Storage Association's Super Van Operator of the Year in Household Goods. He is listed in "America's Registry of Outstanding Professionals," an honor bestowed upon individuals who have demonstrated leadership and dedication in their profession or industry.

Mr. Brady thinks of himself as a small businessperson whose goal is to help other Owner/Operators increase their profitability without increasing their working hours, thereby enabling them to spend more time with their families at home and in their communities. He continues to move forward by staying active in his community and the trucking industry, speaking to organizations and companies, writing industry-specific columns for major trade publications, and continuing to keep in touch with his fellow truckers on the road.

# Other Trucker's University Books from Write up the Road Publishing

ISBN 0-9724026-0-8
**Driven 4 Profits**
*An O/O's Guide to Keeping More of the Money You Earn!*
$ 49.95 + S&H

ISBN 0-9724026-4-0
**Gearing Up 4 Profits**
*An O/O's Guide to Load Profitabilty*
$ 19.95 + S&H

ISBN 0-9724026-8-3
**Quick & Simple Record Keeping System for Owner/Operators**
*Record Keeping Made Simple*
$ 19.95+ S&H

ISBN 0-9724026-9-1
**Load Profit Analysis v2.02**
Companion software to Gearing Up 4 Profits
$139.95 subscription + S&H (includes access to updates through Truckers' University www.truckersu.com)

*Also available:*
**Smart Truckers** Newest Trucking Business CD's
**Oversize Load & Pilot Car Directory**
Plus our latest Truckers' University Books

To order go to: www.truckersbookstore.com
or your other favorite bookstore.

## Strength through Knowledge

Printed in the United States
71458LV00004B/6

9 780972 402682